Published by Writer's Publishing House
info@writerspublishinghouse.com
https://writerspublishinghouse.com

Mamá y yo – Carmichael and Patricia Lewis

ISBN 978-1-64873-155-6

Mi mamá me besa bajo el sol de la mañana.

Mi mamá me besa
al comenzar el día.

Mi mamá reza conmigo mientras nos tocamos las palmas de la mano.

Mi mamá reza conmigo en que todo estará bien en lo cotidiano.

Mi mamá me lee y me hace un sonido chistoso.

Mi mamá me lee antes de jugar con mis juguetes poco vistoso.

Mi mamá me viste,
incluso cuando me paro.

Mi mamá me viste, antes de salir al centro comercial.

Mi mamá me sonríe cuando bailo.

Mi mamá me sonríe,
mientras me río y brinco.

Mi mamá me canta y me ayuda a limpiarme.

Mi mamá me canta, tan encantadora como una reina

Mi mamá me abraza,
me aprieta mucho.

Mi mamá me abraza antes de dar las buenas noches.

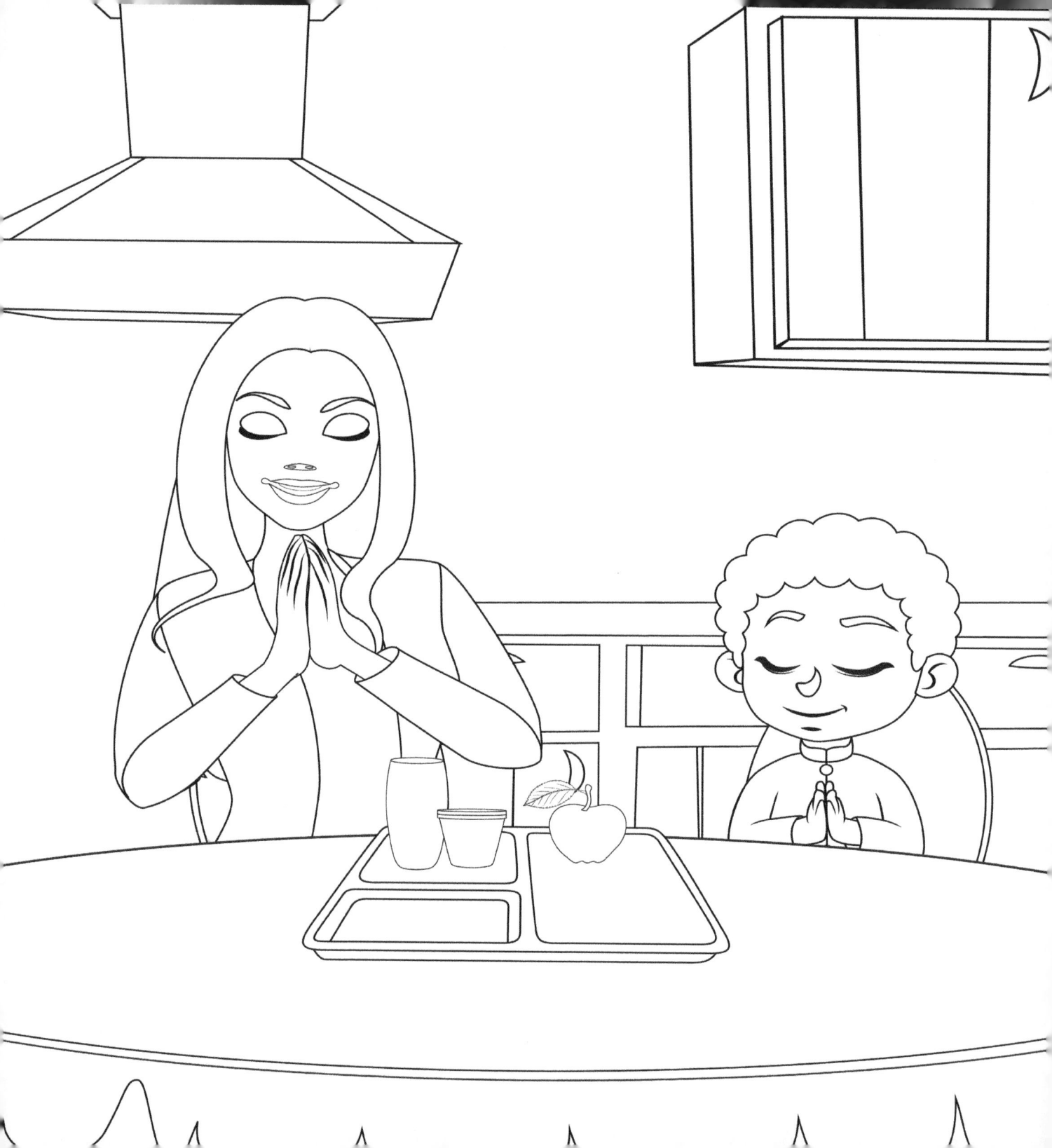

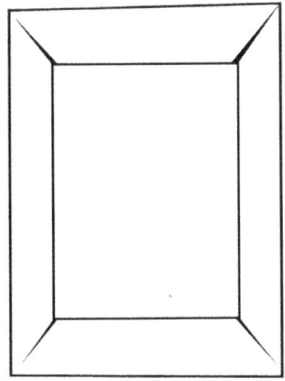

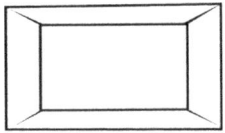

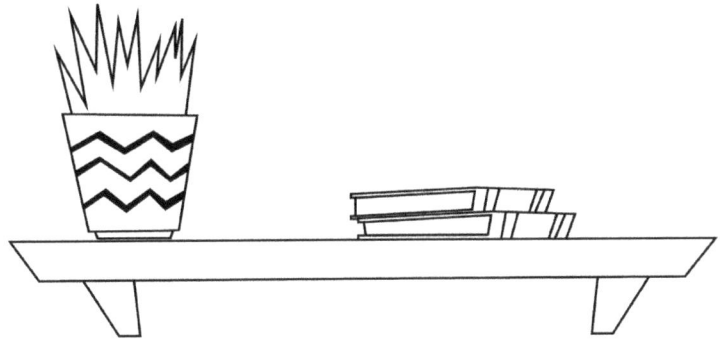

Additional Works from the Author
carmichaellewis.com

Shadows of the Past- *The Path to Greatness*

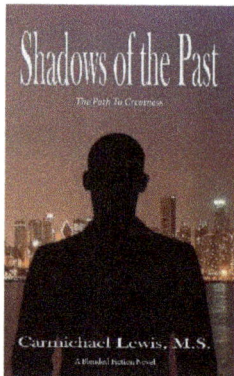

ISBN: 978-1733555135 Paperback

ISBN: 9781648731259 Epub

Julian Parker never prepared himself for the moment that this incredible woman would have walked into his life. Aniyah's presence captivated his soul from the second they met. By their first date, he knew she would be the perfect mate. People always mock love at first sight, but to Julian the disbelief was false. Julian had spent much of his adult-hood running from the past, fighting to free himself from the incidents that had plagued his life.

The newlyweds planned an incredible trip to Hawaii for their honeymoon, and it was an exhilarating time for both parties. Neither one had traveled much, so experiencing the event together made the trip all the more worthwhile. But then the unthinkable happened. Aniyah sat in a hospital room, watching an artificial machine breathe for her husband. The last thing she wanted was to think about traveling when the love of her life was in the hospital.

In the months that follow, joy takes over: Aniyah and Julian celebrate their incredible news. It's as if Julian's heart condition doesn't exist. They want to drag out the experience indefinitely. Julian feels alive for the first time in his life. In the midst of chaos, the couple finds happiness within the smallest package: a baby girl is on the way. As Julian faces the imminent possibility of death, it allows him to dig deep within his soul and confess the overwhelming events of his past. In return, he learns true love is unconditional.

The Ultimate Guide to Teenagers Success: *What They Don't Teach You in School*

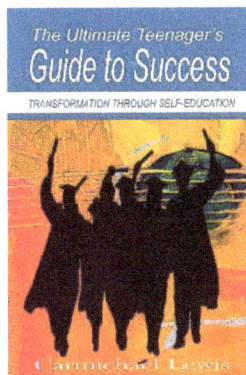

ISBN: 978-1952274008 Paperback

ISBN: 9781952274015 Epub

The Ultimate Teenager's Guide; Transformation through self-education will educate young people on how to set goals to achieve their dreams, how to manage and save their money and how to stay mentally and physically healthy.   With this book, it will help create a vision for their life and help them define what success looks like to them. As young as twelve years old, this book will inspire young people to discover their potential, teach them how to achieve financial independence, and how to succeed in school and beyond. This book will create a breed of healthy and wise adults who will protect the wellbeing of future generations. I sincerely believe that The Ultimate Teenager's Guide will change the trajectory of many teenager's lives for the better.

It is our responsibility as a society to guard the wellbeing of our children. This book is one essential tool that will affect the lives of young people and the community as a whole.

Mira Mira – Look!

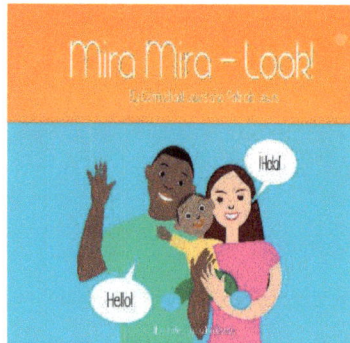

ISBN: 9781647864194 Hardcover

ISBN: 9781647869908 Paperback

ISBN: 9781648731402 Epub

Mira Mira Look is a colorful storybook that introduces Spanish words of everyday household items and phrases. Bilingual books help with language development, recognizing letter sounds and promotes early exploration of other languages. Reading this book with your child will help build vocabulary and observational skills while you bond together.

With bright, bold letters and pictures, Mira Mira - Look is the perfect way to bond with your baby and toddler while exploring Spanish and English words around the house and throughout their day!

Daddy & Me

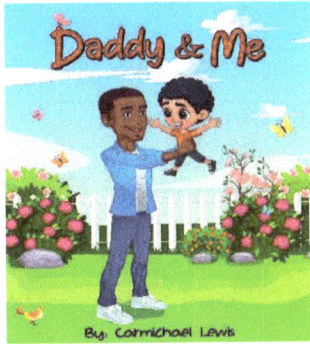

ISBN: 9781648731365 Hardcover

Daddy and Me is a gentle rhyming story told from the perspective of an adored baby boy. Follow Daddy and his son through their day together with your little one. Written intentionally with repetitive phrases and simple rhymes to engage your baby's attention and support cognitive development and recognition of routine.

Papá y yo

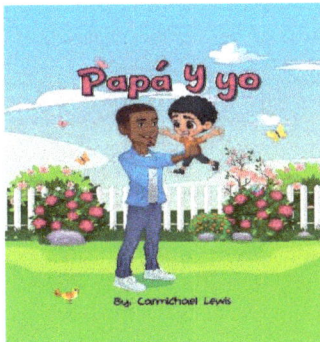

ISBN: 9781648731372 Hardcover

Papá y yo es un cuento de rimas desde la perspectiva de un pequeño bebé. Siga a papá y a su hijo en su día juntos y comparte las atrctivas y coloridas ilustraciones con tu pequeño. Escrito intencionalmente con frases repetitivas y rimas sencillas para captar la atención del bebé y apoyar el desarrollo cognitivo y el reconocimiento de la rutina.

Mommy & Me

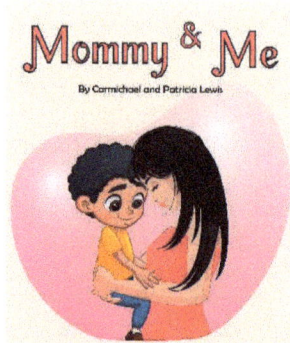

ISBN: 978-1-64873-156-3 Hardcover

Mommy and Me is a sweet story from the perspective of a son describing the daily activity that take place throughout their day. Mommy and Me support children cognitive development with repetitive phrases and simple rhymes to engage their attention.

www.ingramcontent.com/pod-product-compliance
Lightning Source LLC
Chambersburg PA
CBHW040250100426

42811CB00011B/1212